Contents

Preface

During President George W. Bush's campaign for the White House in 2000, he stated, "our [United States of America's] future cannot be separated from the future of Latin America."[1] His campaign promised to improve US relations with Mexico and Latin America while meeting the region's emerging demand for social and economic change. He stated, "should I become the President, I will look south not as an afterthought, but as a fundamental commitment."[2]

Since September 11, 2001, many critics of the Bush administration believed that the US focus on the Global War on Terror (GWOT), also known as the Bush Doctrine, led to a neglect of our neighbors in the Western Hemisphere and contributed to the current crisis in Mexico.[3] With the implementation of the Mérida Initiative in 2008, Mexico became the fifth largest recipient of US foreign aid behind Iraq, Afghanistan, Israel, and Columbia. In light of the increasing demands of GWOT and the current economic crisis in the United States, I became interested in how US tax payer dollars are being spent abroad and if they are achieving the intended goals.

In this research paper, I will assess the potential effectiveness of the Mérida Initiative based on an analysis of the current crisis in Mexico and lessons learned from Plan Columbia. Through the research process, I hope to identify shortcomings in the Mérida Initiative and provide recommendations that can be applied beyond Mexico to enhance security throughout the Western Hemisphere.

---

[1] Alan L. McPherson, *Intimate Ties, Bitter Struggles: The United States and Latin America since 1945,* 1st Edition, Washington: Potomac Books, 2006, 119.
[2] Ibid., 123.

Abstract

President George W. Bush signed the Mérida Initiative, referred to as "Plan Mexico" by critics, into law on June 30, 2008. The plan contains approximately $1.5 billion in aid to Mexico, Central America, and Caribbean countries to improve regional security by reducing organized crime, drug smuggling, and illegal arms trafficking while strengthening domestic institutions. Critics argue that the plan does not adequately address the demand side of the drug model, will add to the militarization of Mexico, empower corrupt institutions, and reduce the rule of law while failing to address the violence of organized crime.[4]

The researcher has identified organized crime, socio-economic disparity, and institutional corruption as the main factors that led Mexican President Calderón to ask for assistance from the United States. Although the Mérida Initiative is a comprehensive plan that attempts to solve a number of complex transnational issues that affect both the United States and Mexico, its performance to date, indicates that it is not meeting its objectives. Using problem-solution methodology, the researcher identified additional measures, such as demand-side drug reduction programs, US gun control enforcement, immigration reform, and economic reforms that would improve the chances of achieving long-term stability and security in the region. The success of the Mérida Initiative will require a holistic and synergistic approach between a joint, interagency, and coalition team.

---

[3] William M. Leogrande, "A Poverty of Imagination: George W. Bush's Policy in Latin America," *Journal of Latin American Studies* 39 (May 2007), 356.

[4] Eric Olsen, "Six Key Issues in United States-Mexico Security Cooperation," Woodrow Wilson International Center for Scholars, July 2008, 3.

Part 1: Introduction

The Mexican government has made the fight on organized crime their top priority. President Felipe Calderón's administration has implemented an aggressive law enforcement strategy against organized crime by utilizing police and military units to reclaim areas once dominated by violence and drug cartels. Additionally, President Calderón has pursued judicial reforms and an overhaul of the federal police force since coming to office in December 2006. In January 2007, President Calderón met with President George W. Bush in Mérida, Mexico, where the two agreed to bilateral and regional cooperation to address organized crime. The main objectives, according to the joint United States and Mexico statement in October 2007, are to maximize the effectiveness of existing efforts of both countries to reduce weapons, human, and drug trafficking along their shared border. Additionally, the Mérida Initiative aims to bolster Mexican and Central American capabilities to identify and interdict criminal gangs, illegal drugs, goods, arms, and people across the region.[1]

Critics of the Mérida Initiative argue that the plan is flawed for four main reasons. First, the war on drugs model that the U.S. is advocating only addresses the supply side. Second, many argue that the US is providing funds and equipment to corrupt police and military forces that will further militarize Mexican society. Third, the plan uses the U.S. counter-terrorism model, enhances executive powers, and represses political opposition. Fourth, the plan fails to adequately address corruption in the political system, police force, military, and judicial system.[2]

Why is the Mérida Initiative important to the United States? According to the US National Security Strategy (NSS), the Western Hemisphere is the "frontline of defense of American national security."[3] The NSS calls for strengthening relations with Mexico and Canada by "bolstering security, strengthening democratic institutions, promoting prosperity, and investing

1

in people."[4] The US National Defense Strategy (NDS) calls for long-term security partnerships to reduce regional instability and prevent transnational crime, safe havens for extremist groups, access to weapons of mass destruction, and a loss of strategic resources for the United States.[5] The US National Military Strategy (NMS) directs the US military to counter threats close to their source and protecting strategic approaches.[6] The Quadrennial Defense Review Report (QDR) calls for integrated security cooperation programs to interact with allies, strengthen their capabilities, and conduct long-duration counter insurgency operations to deter and defend against external transnational threats.[7] It also identifies the importance of a more indirect approach that empowers other states to police themselves and it emphasizes the importance of taking early preventive measures to prevent a crisis from becoming a conflict.[8]

Part 2 of this paper will identify the issues that led President Calderón to ask for assistance from the United States. Part 3 will identify the key aspects of the Mérida Initiative and how the $1.5 billion in Mexican aid will be spent. Part 4 will assess the plan's effectiveness from both the U.S. and Mexican perspectives as well as recommendations to enhance long-term regional security. The author argues that the Mérida Initiative has failed to meet its objectives because it does not address the root cause of the violence along the US-Mexican border. The Mérida Initiative is a comprehensive plan that attempts to solve a number of complex transnational issues that affect both the United States and Mexico. However, its performance to date indicates that it is not meeting its objectives. The success of the Mérida Initiative will require a holistic and synergistic approach between a joint, interagency, and coalition team. It will also require the US to reduce the demand for illegal drugs, reduce the flow of illicit weapons to Mexico, and implement immigration reform. Mexico must continue to pursue economic reform and remove the need for its citizens to choose organized crime over legitimate businesses.

Part 2: Mexico in Crisis

Security Concerns

Despite the Calderón administration's successes in damaging the drug cartels since his election in 2006, the country's security situation continues to deteriorate. As the number of drug seizures and arrests have increased, so have the number of drug-related homicides. Mexico's drug war saw an increase in drug-related homicides from 2,700 in 2007 to nearly 5,000 in 2008.[9] Mexico has also seen an increase in the overall violent nature of these murders with numerous beheadings used to intimidate law enforcement officials and the local populace. The drug war is being fueled by weapons made in the USA and exported to Mexico illegally. In addition to drugs and weapons, the drug cartels are capitalizing on Mexico's poor economic conditions to extort large amounts of cash from individuals wishing to cross the US-Mexican border in search of a job and a better life. The Mérida Initiative has increased the pressure on the drug cartels and has led to greater violence on the US-Mexico border as well as the southwest United States.[10]

Drug Cartels

The United States had over 35 million (12% of the US population) illicit drug users in 2007. The leading drug threat to US society is cocaine, followed by methamphetamines, marijuana, heroin, and pharmaceutical drugs. The US National Drug Threat Assessment for 2009 states that "Mexican Drug Trafficking Organizations (DTOs) represent the greatest organized crime threat to the United States."[11]

Five Mexican drug cartels operate within the United States, Mexico, and Central America. The Gulf Cartel operates from the northeastern Mexican state of Tamaulipas. Osiel Guillen led the Gulf Cartel until his arrest in 2003. They have historically been the most powerful Mexican cartel due in large part to their use of the paramilitary organization called Los Zetas. It is believed that the Los Zetas have been distancing themselves from the Gulf Cartel since Osiel Guillen's extradition to the United States in 2007.[12] The Calderón Administration's recent anti-drug activities have forced the Los Zetas to expand their criminal activities into extortion, kidnapping, and human trafficking.[13]

The Beltran Leyva Cartel has traditionally had an alliance with the Sinaloa Cartel. This relationship, however, was essentially over by the time Alfredo Beltran Leyva was arrested by Mexican authorities in January 2008. Prior to the split, the Beltran Leyva Cartel controlled access to the United States in the Mexican state of Sonora. Since the split, violence has escalated between the two former allies as the Beltran Leyva Cartel quickly secured strategic narcotics transportation routes in seven Mexican states.[14]

The Sinaloa Cartel, headed by Joaquin "El Chapo" Guzman Loera, operates from the Mexican state of Sinaloa. Despite their split from the Beltran Leyva Cartel in 2008 and increased pressure from Mexican law enforcement, the Sinaloa Cartel appears to be the most active smuggler of cocaine. The Sinaloa Cartel has demonstrated the ability to establish operations in Central and South America. They have also reduced their reliance on the US drug market by expanding their supply efforts in Latin America and European countries.[15]

The Vicente Carrillo Fuentes Organization is also known as the Juarez Cartel and operates in the Mexican state of Chihuahua, across the border from El Paso, Texas. The Juarez Cartel has had a long-standing alliance with the Beltran Leyva Cartel, but the organization has recently

4

turned to the Los Zetas to assist them in winning control of Juarez from their former partners, the Sinaloa Cartel. The results of this turf battle have left 2,000 dead in 2008 alone. The Juarez Cartel uses the La Linea, composed of former Chihuahua police officers to control the Mexican side of the border while the Barrio Azteca street gang operates in El Paso, Dallas, and Austin, Texas.[16]

The Arellano Felix Organization, also known as the Tijuana Cartel, has been significantly weakened by efforts from both United States and Mexican law enforcement. The fight for control of the cartel between Fernando "El Ingeniero" Sanchez Zamora and Eduardo Teodoro "El Teo" Garcia Sementa, has left hundreds dead over the past year, including 100 dead during a two week period in October 2008. El Teo has recently received support from the Sinaloa Cartel, which would benefit from controlling access to the United States through Tijuana.[17]

President Calderón's efforts over the past two years are beginning to show results. According to the US National Drug Intelligence Center, the reduction in cocaine seizures in Texas between 2007 and mid-2008 is a result of the difficulty Mexican DTOs are having moving cocaine through Mexico.[18] In 2005, the Mexican government implemented an incremental reduction on the import of ephedrine and pseudoephetamine and other chemicals used for methamphetamine production. In 2007, the Mexican government announced a ban on these chemicals that went into effect in 2008. As a result, methamphetamine production in Mexico and availability in the United States fell in 2007.[19] The Mexican DTOs are attempting to obtain the chemical precursors through South American ports to increase production once again.[20]

Despite the reduction in marijuana seizures along the US-Mexican border, between 2003 and 2005 the high demand for the drug in the United States resulted in a twenty-three percent increase in seizures between 2006 and 2007. The US government estimates that most of the

15,500 metric tons of marijuana produced in Mexico during 2007 was bound for the United States. In an attempt to reduce transportation costs, many of the Mexican DTOs are moving their cannabis operations closer to the US border.[21]

Although heroin use in the United States has remained stable nationally, the Mexican DTO's share of the heroin market is expanding. This expansion is attributed to the reduction in heroin available from Columbia and the Columbian DTOs willingness to relinquish some of their market share to Mexican DTOs in an attempt to decrease their exposure to law enforcement interdiction. As a result, Mexico's heroin production has increased 105 percent from 1999 to 2007.[22]

Illegal Arms Trade

According to a statement released by the Mexican Office of the Attorney General (Procuraduría General de la Republica: PGR) in December 2007, organized crime groups obtain an estimated 8,000 weapons a year from the United States which has led to instability within Mexico.[23] The US Bureau of Alcohol, Tobacco, Firearms, and Explosives (ATF) estimates that ninety percent of the weapons recovered at crime scenes in Mexico originated in the United States. In light of these facts, ATF is working closely with the Mexican government to provide information sharing, training, and technical assistance to reduce illicit weapons.[24]

Despite these initiatives, violent crimes are on the rise in Mexico due in large part to the drug cartels' access to heavy weaponry often obtained from legal outlets in the United States. The drug cartels continue to seek sophisticated weapons in order to maintain an advantage over Mexican security forces. In February 2008, the Mexican army confiscated four tons of weapons in the northeastern state of Tamaulipas. According to Mexican authorities, the shipment included fifty caliber machine guns, plastic explosives, grenades, and assault rifles.[25]

On November 14, 1997, the United States and its partners in the Organization of American States (OAS) signed the Inter American Convention Against the Illicit Manufacturing of and Trafficking in Firearms. This agreement was the first international agreement designed to "prevent, combat, and eradicate illegal trafficking in firearms, ammunition, and explosives." [26] The agreement requires member states to criminalize offenses associated with firearms smuggling, establish licensing procedures, improve border control, and share information that will lead to the capture and prosecution of arms traffickers.[27] Although all of the OAS member states have signed the agreement, only twenty have ratified the convention. Several member states, including the United States, have enacted changes to their laws to comply with the agreement, but the United States' failure to ratify the convention has hindered the full enactment of the provisions.[28]

Human Trafficking

There is an estimated 11-12 million illegal aliens currently living in the United States with approximately 6-7 million coming from Mexico.[29] Ninety percent of Mexican migrants surveyed between 1993 and 1997 said they were going to the US to look for work.[30] The US Federal Bureau of Investigation (FBI) estimates that human trafficking between Mexico and the US earns criminal networks 6 to 9 billion dollars annually. The US Border Patrol estimated that 1.5 million people crossed the US-Mexican border illegally in 2001.[31] The US State Department's Trafficking in Persons Report classifies Mexico as a Tier 2 in 2008 after being on the Tier 2 watch list between 2004 and 2007. Tier 2 states are those states that are not in full compliance with the Trafficking Victims Protection Act's (TVPA) minimum standards, but they are making significant efforts to meet these standards.[32]

Globalization of the world economy has increased the movement of people across borders and created new opportunities for organized crime networks to profit. Because the trafficking of persons generally flows from poorer countries to more wealthier ones, the issue affects Mexico's northern and southern borders.[33] Mexico estimates that approximately 400,000 illegal immigrants cross the Mexican-Guatemalan border each year. President Calderón recently directed an immigration strategy to disrupt criminal organizations along its southern border before they reach Mexico's northern border. Mexico's two main strategies are an increase in law enforcement cooperation with Guatemala on the southern border and a more lenient immigration code.[34]

The United States has attempted to address illegal immigration for the past 10 years with little impact. In 1998, former President Bill Clinton issued a directive establishing a US anti-trafficking strategy aimed at preventing trafficking, protection of victims, and prosecution of violators. In 2002, President Bush signed an executive order establishing an Interagency Task Force to Monitor and Combat Trafficking in Persons.[35] Despite President Bush's call for immigration reform and growing concern over violence on the US-Mexican border, the US Congress has failed to provide an adequate solution.[36] Although the Immigration Reform and Control Act of 1986 contains provisions to punish US employers that hire undocumented workers, the Act has been largely ignored.[37] In September 2006, Congress authorized $1.2 billion to build a 700 km fence along the United States-Mexican border. In March 2007, President Bush promised to accelerate efforts to overhaul immigration law. Bush advocated registration of illegal immigrants and a guest worker program but he met strong opposition in the US Congress.[38]

Insurgent Groups and Gangs

There are two active insurgent groups operating in Mexico that add to the country's level of violence and instability. The first group is the Zapatista National Liberation Army (Ejercíto Zapatistas de Liberación Army: EZLN). The EZLN, founded in 1993, aims to improve the rights of Mexico's indigenous Indian population through constitutional, political, and land reforms. The second group is the Popular Revolutionary Army (Ejercíto Popular Revolucionario: EPR). The EPR, founded in 1996 on a socialist movement, aims to unify various guerilla organizations at the economic, political, and ideological level to obtain representation at the legislative level. Despite the inability of these Marxist-based organizations to overthrow the state military, they both use hit-and-run tactics to gain publicity for their respective causes.[39] Since 2006, these groups have elevated the violence in response to President Calderón's deployment of state security and military forces to lawless areas of Mexico. The EPR claimed responsibility for a bombing near Mexico City's Federal Security Ministry on 15 February 2008 and attacks on Mexico's oil and gas pipelines on 7 May 2008.[40,41]

In addition to the insurgent groups, gangs are a growing problem in Mexico with some 15,000 gang members operating in 20 Mexican states.[42] There are three major gangs operating in the United States, Mexico, and Central America. The Mexican Mafia is one of the most dominant and oldest US prison gangs.[43] The two most violent gangs are the "18th Street" (M-18) and the Mara Salvatrucha (MS-13) that originated in Los Angeles, California. Mexican immigrants formed M-18 in the 1960s and Salvadorans formed M-13 in the 1980s. M-13 has an estimated 10,000 members in 33 US states. Due to US immigration policy, many of these gang members were deported to their home countries in the mid-1990s. Between 2000 and 2004, the US deported 20,000 criminals to Central America. These gang members turn to crime in their home countries due in large part to poverty, urbanization, and stagnant job markets. Mexico and

Central American countries have lacked the required resources to address the social, political, and economic issues that are the root cause of gang violence.[44] Max G. Manwaring of the Strategic Studies Institute calls street gangs the "New Urban Insurgency."[45] According to Manwaring, these gangs create instability that could destroy democracy and free market economies "one street or neighborhood at a time."[46]

Government Institutions

Corruption is defined as the abuse of public power for personal gain.[47] Mexico, like many nations around the world, is battling corruption that has undermined the authority and legitimacy of their democratic institutions. Members of Mexico's law enforcement agencies and criminal justice system claim that they strictly enforce and impartially apply the rule of law. Amnesty International refutes these claims and states that their independence and impartiality are undermined by poor pay, limited resources, lack of training, excessive work-load, and political interference.[48]

Police

Mexican police fall into two general categories at all levels of government. The preventative police (Policía Preventive) are uniformed police officers that are responsible for preventing crimes by providing security through presence. They may detain individuals that they catch in the act of a crime, but they do not normally participate in serving arrest warrants. Once a crime has been committed, the investigative police (Policía Judicial-"Judiciales"-or Policía Ministerial) are the non-uniformed police officers that are responsible for conducting investigations and executing arrest warrants for the prosecutor's office.[49]

Each Mexican state and the Federal District of Mexico City have their own preventative and judicial police forces. Mexico also has two federal police agencies. The Federal Preventative Police (Policía Federal Preventiva, PFP), created in 1999 to prevent federal crimes, and the Federal Investigative Agency (Agencia Federal de Investigaciones, AFI) investigates federal crimes for the Federal Attorney General's Office. The AFI replaced the corrupt Federal Judicial Police (Policía Judicial Federal, PJF) in 2002.[50] In 2007, the AFI and PFP were brought under the Federal Police (Policía Federal) to unify their chains of command, increase their capabilities, improve coordination, and avoid information leaks.[51]

Mexico has 407,000 police officers that are employed by more than 3,000 different police agencies at the local, state, and federal level.[52] This equates to one police officer for every 270 people in Mexico. The United States, in comparison, has 837,000 police officers in nearly 18,000 police agencies.[53] This equates to one police officer for every 363 people. Per capita, Mexico has a larger police force than the United States.

The quality of these police forces varies based on the state, region, or municipality. Some are on par with other developed countries and others suffer from incompetence, corruption, and divided loyalties between local elites and criminal organizations.[54] The main problem confronting Mexican officials is the corruption within the police force. There are four main reasons for police corruption. First, they have no minimum education requirement so most police officers are poorly educated with an elementary school education or less. The second major issue is training. Institutional support for training has remained relatively poor across the 58 Mexican police academies and a new recruit receives an average of just 4.5 months of training. Their training has not provided them with an understanding of human rights and community relations. Additionally, most police agencies lack guidelines and the tools to

11

effectively evaluate job performance.[55] The last two issues confronting the Mexican police force are low pay and a lack of resources. These issues create an environment that leads to corruption.

In a 2002 survey conducted by Transparency International, the average Mexican household spent 8 percent of their annual income on bribes.[56] President Calderón has increasingly used the military to take over law enforcement duties in towns suspected of substantial police corruption. In March 2007, Mexican federal police and the military raided the Tabasco state police following the attempted assassination of Tabasco's head of public security. Federal investigators suspected that the assassination attempt was conducted by a network of current and former police officers connected to organized crime and drug trafficking in Tabasco.[57] In December 2007, Mexican authorities took a similar action in Rosarita, a town just south of Tijuana, in the state of Baja California, following the assassination of the local police chief.[58] According to a news release by Mexico's National Public Security System in February 2008, 1,400 police officers were given reliability tests that included polygraphs and drug testing. These tests reinforced corruption concerns when sixty percent of the officers failed their polygraphs.[59]

In October 2008, the Mexican government uncovered the most serious penetration of its law enforcement structure in over a decade. Mexico's chief federal prosecutor announced that the country's top anti-drug official was being paid by the Juarez Cartel and top officials at the organized crime division of the chief federal prosecutor's office were being paid by the Sinaloa Cartel. Officials estimate that these individuals were receiving between US$150-450 thousand dollars per month for classified information regarding anti-drug agents and operations. Although the investigation is still on-going, officials believe that these individuals were a part of a ring of corrupt officials from the federal police force, the Mexican Interpol, and the US embassy.[60]

Military

The Mexican military's primary roles are internal security and civil support. Since Mexico lacks any significant external threat, they have traditionally spent less than one-half of one percent of their gross domestic product (GDP) on defense. As a result, the majority of their military inventory has become nearly obsolete. President Calderón increased the defense budget by twenty-five percent in 2007 and thirteen percent in 2008 in an attempt to improve the military's capabilities. Although these expenditures are significant, they amount to just 0.46 percent of Mexico's GDP in 2008.[61]

In addition to modernizing their equipment, the Mexican military has invested heavily in professionalizing their institutions. In the last decade, Mexico has implemented professional development schools, at all ranks, that are prerequisites for future promotions. Additionally, they have incorporated human rights training and published rules of engagement to reduce the number of rights violations during civil operations.[62]

Prior to President Vicente Fox's election in 2000, the Mexican military's role in politics and policy-making were non-existent. With the increasing role of the Mexican military in domestic affairs, President Fox encouraged all military services to participate in inter-institutional debates that increased the Military's role in policy decisions and interagency cooperation.[63] Although the Mexican president has extensive powers over the employment of the Mexican military, the increase in interaction has provided greater civilian oversight of military affairs.[64]

The democratization of Mexico has also provided more transparency within the military. In 2003, President Fox enacted the Law of Access to Information that requires the military to disclose information to the public. The military has also attempted to reduce the risk of corruption by rotating its officers regularly between garrisons to prevent the development of relationships with criminal elements at any one location. As a result, the Mexican people have shown more confidence in their military than any other national institution.[65]

Since December 2006, President Calderón has deployed nearly 30,000 federal troops and police throughout the country. The Mexican army has taken over law enforcement duties in half of its 31 states due to the extensive infiltration of the drug cartels in the local security forces.[66] Calderón's Administration is credited with 5,800 arrests and the seizure of 2,900 tons of marijuana and 24 tons of cocaine, worth an estimated $20 billion US dollars during his first eighteen months in office.[67] Despite these successes, Calderón has come under criticism from the Mexican congress as well as international organizations that believe that law enforcement duties should remain in the civil sector.[68] Many argue that Mexico's use of the military has weakened civilian institutions and eroded the barriers built to prevent the military's involvement in politics.[69] Although the government's primary duty is to protect its citizens, the government's use of the military against its own people can create the appearance of old traditions of military control and authoritarianism that are not compatible with democracy.[70]

Traditionally, the US State Department provided aid to foreign militaries. In recent years, Combatant Commanders have taken a greater role due in large part to the amount of resources these commands bring to the region. The United States foreign policy has further blurred the lines between civilian and military roles since September 11, 2001, with the introduction of the term "narco-terrorism."[71] In 2006, the Bush Administration called for the "Global Train and Equip" authority in FY2006's National Defense Authorization Act, to provide the US Department of Defense the funds necessary to train military forces because the US State Department's security assistance process was viewed as "too slow and cumbersome."[72]

The use of the Mexican military in civil law enforcement actions has had negative impacts as well. The Mexican Commission Rights publicly stated that the military was involved in abuses such as rape, illegal searches, and illegal detentions due to their lack of training in civilian law enforcement. The legitimacy of local and state governments are undermined following a military intervention because the public perceives them as either incompetent or corrupt. The increased number of military deaths has also increased the number of military deserters. The Mexican government estimates that there were 30,000 desertions per year from 2002 to 2006. In 2007, the number was down to 17,000. Additionally, the use of the military in the counter-narcotics effort is likely to lead to corruption within the institution, much as it did in the police force. Although national polls show that most Mexicans want the military involved in anti-drug activities, public support has shown a decline in the states where the military has conducted operations.[73]

Judicial System and the Rule of Law

According to the US State Department, Mexico's federal government generally respects and promotes human rights at the federal level, but impunity and corruption remain problems at the state and local levels. Human rights violations in 2007 included unlawful killings by security forces, police kidnappings, poor and overcrowded prisons, arbitrary arrests and detentions, violence against women, coerced confessions, intimidation of journalists intended to invoke self-censorship, discrimination against indigenous people, child labor and corruption, inefficiency, and lack of transparency in the judicial system.[74]

Since 2004, the Mexican government has shown its commitment to human rights by signing and ratifying the majority of international human rights agreements. The main obstacle in implementing these changes is the failure of Mexico's 31 states to adopt and abide by these

15

international treaties. In accordance with Mexican law, the international human rights treaties fall between the Mexican constitution and federal and state law, therefore, the treaties are generally not applied at the state level and judicial rulings rarely consider them.[75]

Legislative reforms initiated during the 1990s are beginning to take hold in the judicial branch of the Mexican government. Since these reforms were implemented, the executive branch has gradually reduced its influence over the judicial system. Despite these efforts, however, a 2001 UN Special Rapporteur found that the judicial branch still lacked autonomy and independence to effectively carry out its duties.[76]

In 2008, Mexico adopted constitutional reforms relating to public security and the criminal justice system that will be implemented over the next eight years. In addition to legislative initiatives, Mexico also establishment the Office of the High Commissioner for Human Rights in Mexico and created a National Human Rights Program at the federal level. Mexico has also established human rights units in the army, public prosecutor's office, and police forces to train personnel and investigate reported violations. Although these changes indicate Mexico is committed to improving human rights and the rule of law, they will have little impact if the 31 state legislatures fail to incorporate these changes into state law.[77]

Political System

Mexico's political system was dominated by the Institutional Revolutionary Party (Partido Revolucionario Institucional, PRI) since 1938. The PRI was founded on a revolutionary nationalistic ideology that appealed to workers and peasants. The PRI has traditionally maintained a national power base because of their emphasis on state power, political authority, and law and order. Their supporters were primarily the uneducated, rural population that had little exposure to the mainstream media. The party's implementation of neoliberal economic reforms in the 1990s led to their loss of power in the Chamber of Deputies in 1997 and the Presidency in 2000.[78]

The other two political parties in Mexico are the National Action Party (Partido Acción Nacional, PAN) and the Party of the Democratic Revolution (Partido de la Revolución Democrática, PRD). The PAN is a conservative party that performs best in more industrial, educated, and urban areas. The PRD is a leftist party that attracts people that fall between the PRI and PAN demographics, in areas with some education but a weak manufacturing base. The success of both of these parties is a result of their ability to widen their platforms in order to gain support from marginal voters during Mexico's democratic transition over the past 15 years.[79]

Mexico's peaceful transition of power from the PRI to the PAN following 71 years of single party rule was a significant event in Mexican politics. President Fox made good on his anti-corruption campaign pledges by pushing the Freedom of Information (FOI) Act through the legislature in 2003. According to José Octavio López Presa, the former executive director for Transparency International in Mexico, anti-corruption measures have been effective at the federal level. At the state level, the FOI has had less of an impact due in part to the requirement of individuals to request information in person because states lack an internet-based request system.[80]

Despite these successes by President Fox, public distrust remains throughout Mexico due in large part to a lack of political reform. The current political institutions were effective under the PRI's 71-year reign because the President maintained the majority of power. Today, constitutional changes have led to more power sharing between the President and Congress, but representation of the people within these institutions is still lacking. Two hundred of the five hundred seats in the Chamber of Deputies, the lower house of the Mexican Congress, are appointed by party elites rather than elected by their constituents. Additionally, the Mexican constitution limits presidential and congressional officials to just one term. The combination of political appointments and one term limits further erodes a politician's commitment to their constituents.[81]

The Mexican political system was tested again during the 2006 presidential election between PAN's Felipe Calderón and the PRD's López Obrador. The Federal Electoral Institution (IFE), responsible for organizing, counting votes, and resolving voting issues at the federal level, declared President Calderón the winner by a margin of just 250,000 votes (0.58%). The Electoral Court of the Federal Judicial Power (TEPJF) that reviews the IFE's decisions upheld the verdict. Despite this success, the election of President Calderón with just 35% of the popular vote highlights the need for further political reform within Mexico. A run-off election, for example, would have provided the winner more legitimacy among a majority of the population.[82]

Economy

Although Mexico's economy is relatively small in comparison to the United States, their economy has become more closely tied to the United States since the North American Free Trade Agreement was signed in 1994. The United States is Mexico's top trading partner and Mexico is the United States' second-largest trading partner behind Canada. Thirty-two percent of Mexico's gross domestic product (GDP) comes from exports and 85% of these go to the United States.[83] Mexicans working in the United States sent $16.6 billion, 2% of Mexico's GDP, in remittance payments to family members in Mexico during 2004.[84] Mexico is the sixth largest oil producer in the world and second in the Western Hemisphere behind the United States. In addition to oil reserves, the country has a substantial amount of natural gas and minerals.[85] Mexico received $966 million in US aid between 1997 and 2007.[86] The United

States invested $92 billion, 3% of US foreign investments, in the Mexican economy in 2007.[87] Despite economic freedoms, foreign investment, international aid, and the abundance of resources, Mexico continues to lag behind the United States in many key economic indicators.

With a population one-third the size of the United States, Mexico has a GDP and per capita GDP that equate to just 6% and 16% of the United States' GDP, respectively.[88] The Mexican government receives one-third of its budget from the state-owned oil company, Petroleos Mexicanos (Pemex). With oil production in decline at Mexico's Cantarell oil field, the Mexican Congress was forced to provide Pemex with additional funds for oil exploration in 2007.[89] The importance of oil and other state-owned energy companies is a cause for concern. President Calderón has invested heavily in the fight against organized crime, but many Mexicans are still waiting to see if the government will reform the energy, telecommunications, and transportation monopolies that they believe are undermining the free market, competition, and job growth.[90]

Part 3: Mérida Initiative

Title I and II: Assistance to Mexico and Countries of Central America

Law Enforcement

The Mérida Initiative provided approximately $271.6 million to Mexico for law enforcement in 2008. The money was spent on aircraft that conduct aerial interdiction of drugs, arms, and other illicit cargo. Mexico refurbished and upgraded sensors (radar, forward-looking infrared, and computers) on two of its existing Cessna Citation II 550s and spend $104 million to buy eight Bell 412 EP helicopters for the Mexican Air Force. They spent $100 million for two new Casa 235s to complement the Navy's seven Casa 212s and 6 Casa 235s already in maritime surveillance service. A portion of these funds bought the federal police force (SSP), Army, and customs agents ion scanner (non-intrusive inspection equipment (NIIE) to detect illicit drugs, weapons, and explosives. The Mexican Telecommunication and Transportation Secretariat (SCT) received $25.3 million for satellite communications, the design of Mexico's next generation of satellite communications, and enhancements to Mexico's mail handling and screening capabilities. Law enforcement received mobile gamma ray machines, x-ray vans, training of canine teams, 30 armored cars, 200 bulletproof vests/helmets, and radios. Additional radios, protective gear, computers, vehicles, and tracking/surveillance equipment were provided to special anti-gang, anti-organized crime and money laundering units.[91] In FY09, Mexico will receive $206 million for two additional Casa 235s for the Mexican Navy and three UH-60s for the Secretariat of Public Security (SSP). The SSP is currently buying four UH-60s on their own to compliment the 19 UH-1s and the 11 Schweitzer aircraft that provide a rapid mobility capability. The remainder of the money will used to purchase three Cessna Caravans, mobile gamma ray machines, x-ray vans, and train canine teams for the SSP. [92]

The Mérida Initiative provided approximately $30.1 million to Central America in 2008. $15 million was used for law enforcement equipment upgrades and to establish a polygraph program to vent sensitive investigative units (SIU) that work with the DEA. It also establish a Central America Fingerprint Exchange (CAFÉ) that will be linked to the FBI. Two million dollars went to refurbish 65- and 82-foot patrol boats for Costa Rica's Coast Guard. Over three million dollars was used to establish a Spanish version of e-trace software to track illicit weapons, ATF interdiction training, an ATF advisor, and a small arms and light weapons collection and destruction program. Five million dollars went to the transnational anti-gang initiative (TAG) in the form of computers, software, protective gear and equipment. Two million dollars went to the International Law Enforcement Academy (ILEA), that trains 700 police officers annually, in criminal justice, law enforcement, and the rule of law. [93]

Intelligence

Mexico received $14.9 million in FY08 and $13.3 million in FY09 for intelligence purposes. Over six million funded the PGR's Operation against Smugglers (and traffickers) Initiative on Safety and Security (OASISS). The money provided software and e-mail upgrades to allow secure communications between US-Mexican border authorities to help identify, investigate, prioritize, and prosecute cross-border criminal activity. These funds provided the Mexican Intelligence service with computers, software, database, VOIP, and connectivity between the National Security and Investigation Center (CISEN) and 18 points of entry (POE). Additionally, funds provided forensic computer analysis equipment to interpret digital evidence from computers seized by law enforcement and the computer infrastructure for financial intelligence

21

functions. Five million dollars went to the Financial Intelligence Unit in the form of hardware and software to fight money laundering and provide information sharing.[94] Central America received one million dollars in FY08 for intelligence purposes. This money provided software for an internet-based information and intelligence program that will link 48 countries together under the DEA's Center for Drug Intelligence (CDI) Program.[95]

Customs and Immigration

Mexico received $61.5 million in FY08 and $69.9 million in FY09 for customs and immigration purposes. $61.5 million was given to Mexico's National Migration Institute (INAMI) for passport and fingerprint readers, communication, medical supplies, and search and rescue equipment. The funds were used to purchase computers and software to track personnel entering and exiting Mexico from its 165 POEs (58 air, 51 sea, and 56 land). The software will digitize forms and permits to speed the customs process as well as provide links to US customs and law enforcement agencies. Mexican customs received over $70 million for NIIE and a dog/handler training program that will create 300 canine teams and 100 kennels around the country. This includes $6.5 million for a NIIE central maintenance facility.[96] Central America received six million dollars in FY08 for customs and immigration purposes. They received two million for NIIE, 1.7 million for aviation security, port security, and document fraud prevention, and $2.3 million for a repatriation notification system that will be linked to the US Department of Homeland Security and the FBI fingerprint database.[97]

Judicial Institutions

Mexico received $86.2 million in FY08 and $37.3 million in FY09 for judicial reforms. The Mexican Attorney General's Office (PGR) received the majority of these funds with $28.8 million to create a unified and integrated information infrastructure to make the PGR more transparent, accountable, and reduce corruption while enhancing public confidence. They received $13.5 million to modernize equipment in the PGR's forensic laboratory and $29.2 million for software that will enhance case tracking, the penal process, intelligence analysis, and data dissemination by linking 32 sub offices with headquarters. They also received another $2.5 million to reengineer their human resources and financial management systems.[98]

The judicial system received two million dollars for judicial reform efforts of penal codes and criminal procedure codes to bring Mexico in compliance with anti-corruption standards set in the UN Convention Against Corruption (UNCAC) and the Inter-American Convention Against Corruption (IACAC). The police, prosecutors, and prison officials received $3.5 million worth of human rights training and the bar association will receive one million dollars to implement judicial reforms in law school curriculums. Fifteen million dollars was spent on courts-management and prosecutorial capacity-building. The Clerk of the Court system will help standardize and centralize case administration and limit opportunities for corruption. This system will also provide judicial statistics such as caseloads, pre-trial detention rates, and promote judicial efficiency. Training will also include surveillance, under-cover operations, and forensic evidence to strengthen the prosecutor's ability to prosecute complex criminal cases. The judicial system received four million dollars for alternative case resolution training at the state and local level that will free up the courts for higher priority cases. Additional funding is provided for prison management, a witness protection program, and extradition, evidence handling, and chain of custody training.[99] Central America received six million dollars in FY08 to improve the criminal justice system in the form of courts management, prosecutor capacity building, and prison management.[100]

Anti-Corruption Measures

Mexico received $12.5 million in FY08 and $1.3 million in FY09 for anti-corruption programs. Seven million dollars went to police professionalization training and the establishment of Citizen Complaint centers. These centers will act as a watchdog agency for Mexico's Office of the Inspector General (OIG). Funds are allocated to strengthen the OIG and SSP's internal integrity mechanisms to increase public confidence in law enforcement. Funds will also be used to establish a culture of lawfulness program for schools, law enforcement and other parts of civil society. These programs are intended to partner the public with law and judicial institutions as an accountability mechanism to maintain public order, the rule of law and responsiveness to the citizen's concerns. Two million dollars has been allocated to improve law enforcement's capability to administer polygraphs to its own personnel to identify corrupt police officers. Central America received one million dollars in FY08 for police professionalization to build public confidence.[101]

Non-Governmental Organizations (NGOs) and Institutions

Mexico received $16.1 million in FY08 and $12.9 million in FY09 for NGOs and civil society programs. Thirty million dollars is dedicated to drug awareness, demand reduction, and rehabilitation programs. Three million dollars will be used for training NGOs on the code of criminal procedures, human rights laws, and the criminal justice system. In FY09, funds will be utilized to create citizen advisory boards to monitor citizen complaint centers and serve as internal oversight bodies. These funds will strengthen the NGOs ability to educate the Mexican public on their rights and document any violations. Central America received five million dollars in FY08 for anti-gang strategy and prevention.[102]

Title III: Administrative Provisions

Title III provides guidance that the aid to Mexico and Central America is contingent on human rights performance. All individuals receiving aid must be vetted to ensure they have not committed human rights violations in the past. Anyone receiving aid who commits a human rights violation must be investigated and prosecuted by civilian authority. This measure is waiverable if the state demonstrates it is making significant progress to eliminate such violations. Equipment and material provided in the initiative must be used for its intended purpose and all equipment must be tracked and accounted for in annual reports. This title also limits US civilian contractors supporting the initiative to a maximum of 50 in Mexico and 100 in Central America without a Presidential waiver. This aid is in addition to all other aid programs currently in effect and it does not alter the US Arms Export Control Act.[103]

Title IV: Support Activities in the United States

Title IV recognizes that supply-side drug reduction measures do not work alone and tasks the President to submit his plan for intensifying demand-side strategies within 180 days. This title also recognizes the need to stop the flow of weapons from the US to Mexico and Central America. It authorizes the ATF to add 25 special agents and 15 inspectors to Project Gunrunner. It tasks the Attorney General and the ATF to intensify their drug enforcement efforts with additional agents, to provide one initiative team per border state, and increase their coordination with other law enforcement agencies. It also authorizes $15 million per year in FY08-FY10 for Attorney General's Gunrunner and provides $9.5 million per year to enhance cross border cooperation. It also recognizes the need to stop chemical precursors.[104]

Title V: Miscellaneous Provisions

Title V tasks the Department of State to appoint a high-level coordinator, rank and status of an ambassador, to conduct interagency planning, coordination, and execution in support of the Mérida Initiative. It also emphasizes the importance of building civilian security institutions, enhancing the rule of law, protection of human rights, accountability, oversight and monitoring mechanisms, and metrics. This title tasks the President to provide metrics in a report to congress 60 days after the bill is signed into law. This report will include indicators on the long-term effectiveness of the equipment and training, narcotics arrests, interdicted drug shipments, police reform, quantity of drug supply reduction, cross-utilization of equipment, school attendance, prevention program attendance, and level of cooperation between US, Mexico, and Central American law enforcement agencies. The President is also required to provide a report 180 days after the bill is signed and then once annually. This report includes metrics, assessment of coordination, status of equipment (transfers, utilization, training), human rights, assessment of the equipment's effectiveness, Mexico's public security strategy, flow of illegal arms, use of contractors, Central America Regional Security Plan, status of phasing the military out of law enforcement, displacement and diversion of drug trafficking patterns, and impact on border violence and security. The Mérida Initiative will expire on June 10, 2010.[105]

Part 4: Conclusions and Recommendations

The security environment in the Western Hemisphere is unique because every country, except Cuba, is democratic. This is significant because democracies tend to look out for the welfare of their people, maintain stable relationships, and do not wage war with their neighbors.[106] The primary threats in the Western Hemisphere have evolved from the communist and autocratic rule of 25 years ago to the terrorism, narco-trafficking, money laundering, gunrunning, and human trafficking of today.[107] Despite the expansion of free trade and democracy in the region, the Western Hemisphere's "Zone of Peace" is threatened by transnational criminal organizations and domestic insurgencies. The events of September 11, 2001, demonstrated that the United States has vulnerabilities that need to be addressed in order to provide security for its citizens.[108] Globalization and information technology have added additional challenges to the security environment as societies become more interwoven. In order to enhance security and stability throughout the Western Hemisphere, the United States must develop a holistic and well-coordinated strategic approach that considers the social, economic, and political factors that are unique to Mexico and the other Latin American countries.[109]

Although the United States and Mexico have cooperated in the past, the Mexican government has always handled the relationship with caution due to the massive land seizure by the United States following the Mexican-American War from 1846 to 1848.[110] Since the election of President Fox in 2000 and President Calderón in 2006, the relationship between these two countries has drastically improved due in large part to free trade agreements and shared security concerns. The conditions in Mexico today are much like the conditions that existed in Columbia for the past decade. Since 2000, the United States has provided over $2.5 billion in aid for Plan Columbia. Although Plan Columbia has not resolved all of Columbia's issues, it is arguably an overall success. With US assistance, Columbia has reduced the influence of insurgents, corruption, and related violence while strengthening their standards of governance, human rights, the rule of law, and economic policies.[111] Since 2002, Columbia kidnapping rate has dropped by 83 percent and their murder rate has dropped by 40 percent.[112] Despite these successes, Plan Columbia has failed to reduce coca cultivation by 50% over the first 6 years of the plan.[113] The Office of National Drug Control Policy reported in 2005 that "despite massive spraying of coca fields, the area of coca cultivation remained 'statistically unchanged.'"[114] The Mérida Initiative, in contrast, is a comprehensive approach that provides equipment, training, and information technology to enhance Mexico's law enforcement capabilities while improving governance, institutions, and the rule of law. The Mérida Initiative, like Plan Columbia, will enhance US-Mexican security, but is not the solution in and of itself.

Plan Columbia teaches important lessons that will improve the effectiveness of the Mérida Initiative. The primary concern for both the US and Mexico is reducing the violence. The violence is fueled by the demand for drugs in the United States and the poor economic conditions in Mexico. The flow of illicit weapons, human trafficking, and corruption are a result of these two factors. The United States' counter-drug budget has declined by 21% since 2002 while spending over 60% of it on supply-side programs that fail to address the long-term, root cause of the drug problem.[115]

The United States needs to revise its arms control policies and procedures to reduce the illicit arms going south. The United States should ratify the OAS Firearms Convention to boost the agreement's credibility. Failure to ratify this convention will continue to erode the United States' influence in the hemisphere and universal implementation of the provisions.[116] The ratification of this agreement will require few changes to US law, pose no real threat to lawful gun ownership, and require few costs in terms of dollars and time to implement. The reduction in illicit weapons and the good will generated by the US support of a multilateral agreement will pay for themselves.[117] Additionally, the US must increase the number of inspection of vehicles crossing into Mexico to prevent large shipments of weapons making their way to the cartels.

Financial reform in Mexico is another important aspect of reducing the socio-economic disparity in Mexico. Mexico needs an annual growth rate of 5 percent to employ 1 million new workers joining the labor pool. Mexico has made important steps towards improving economic conditions over the past decade, but more is required to reduce poverty and the desire to participate in the drug trade. Reforms in the energy and telecommunications sectors, high manufacturing taxes, rigid labor laws, and poor infrastructure have increased production costs and diverted investment.[118]

Although the Mérida Initiative is a comprehensive approach, 80% of the aid is going to law enforcement type functions while only 20% is going to institution building and the rule of law. Once the security situation improves, the US and Mexico need to relook this mix to ensure the institutions that will provide long-term stability are well established. Mexico has taken a number of steps to improve the judicial system, reduce corruption, and improve human rights at the federal level, but more are needed at the state and local level.

An initial failure of Plan Columbia was the Columbian government's lack of a strategic level plan to deal with their narco-insurgent-paramilitary problem. It is imperative that the United States and Mexico obtain a consensus among political, economic, and military leaders to develop a coherent plan that provides direction and timely guidance.[119] Title V of the Mérida Initiative tasks the Department of State to serve as the US lead agency for planning, coordinating, and executing the provisions outlined in the initiative. The US Department of State should provide an overarching, hemispheric approach that ties Plan Columbia, the Andean Initiative, the Mérida Initiative, and the Security and Prosperity Partnership of North America (SPP) together.[120] A hemispheric approach will maximize resources and reduce redundancy across US agencies and instruments of national power. Greater cooperation and integration of regional security cooperation plans is also needed between US Northern Command and US Southern Command. The US Navy's Four Fleet, re-establishing under US Southern Command in April 2008, will enhance regional security and demonstrate a greater commitment to regional partners.[121]

In summary, the Mérida Initiative is a comprehensive plan that attempts to solve a number of complex transnational issues that affect both the United States and Mexico. Both countries, however, need to take additional measures to improve the chances of achieving long-term stability and security in the region. Although drug prevention programs, institution building, and intergovernmental coordination are imperative, the most important measure that both countries must possess is patience. Plan Columbia began as a 6-year program and is nearly a decade old. The Mérida Initiative began as a 3-year program, but it is likely to go much longer. To prevent another endless US program, the US Department of State must assess the Mérida Initiative's progress frequently by measuring the program's effectiveness against the metrics specified by the President of the United States. Since the Mérida Initiative is only 9 months old, the author did not have the data to assess the performance of the plan against these metrics. An annual assessment of these metrics would greatly benefit the implementation of the Mérida Initiative in the future.

Notes

[1] Laura Carlsen, "A Primer on Plan Mexico," Americas Policy Program Special Report , Washington, DC: Center for International Policy (May 5, 2008, updated July 10, 2008), 4.

[2] Eric Olsen, "Six Key Issues in United States-Mexico Security Cooperation," Woodrow Wilson International Center for Scholars (July 2008), 3.

[3] Office of the President of the United States, *The National Security Strategy of the United States of America* (Washington, D.C., March 2006), 37.

[4] Ibid.

[5] US Department of Defense, *National Defense Strategy of the United States of America* (Washington, D.C., June 2008), 9.

[6] US Department of Defense, *National Military Strategic Plan for the War on Terrorism* (Washington DC: Office of the Secretary of Defense, 2006), 4-12.

[7] US Department of Defense, *Quadrennial Defense Review Report* (Washington, DC: Department of Defense, February 2006), 37-38.

[8] Ibid., 17-18.

[9] "Mexican Drug Cartels: Government Progress and Growing Violence," *Stratfor* (December 11, 2008), 15.

[10] *Stratfor*, "Mexican Drug Cartels," 16.

[11] US Department of State, *Trafficking In Persons Report*, The White House (Washington, D.C., June 2008), III.

[12] *Stratfor*, "Mexican Drug Cartels," 4.

[13] Ibid., 5.

[14] Ibid.

[15] Ibid., 6-7.

[16] Ibid., 7-8.

[17] Ibid., 8-9.

[18] US Department of State, *Trafficking In Persons Report* , 4.

[19] Ibid., 9.

[20] Ibid., 16.

[21] Ibid., 21-22.

[22] Ibid., 27-28.

[23] "Mexico's Destabilized by Weapons from US" *Jane's Intelligence Review*, (December 11, 2007), 1.

[24] US Embassy Mexico City, "Combating Illicit Firearms" (September 2008), 1.

[25] Oscar Beccera, "Firing Line – Tracking Mexico's Illegal Weapons," *Jane's Intelligence Review* (May 15, 2008), 1.

[26] "OAS Convention Against Illicit Firearms Trafficking Fact Sheet," The White House, Office of the Press Secretary (November 14, 1997), 1.

[27] Robert Sherman, "The Real Terrorist Missile Threat and What Can Be Done About It," *Federation of American Scientists* 56, no. 3 (Autumn 2003), 17.

[28] Matthew Schroeder, *Small Arms, Terrorism, and the OAS Firearms Convention*, *Federation of American Scientist,* Occasional Paper No. 1 (March 2004) 33.

[29] Sidney Weintraub, "The Fence as a Metaphor for How the United States Views Its Relations with Mexico," *Issues In International Political Economy* 82 (Washington, D.C.: Center for Strategic and International Studies, October 2006), 1-2.

Notes

[30] Jorge I. Domínguez and Rafael Fernández de Castro, *The United States and Mexico: Between Partnership and Conflict* (New York: Routledge, 2001) 149.

[31] Oscar Becerra, "Mexican People-Smuggling Trade Worth Billions," *Jane's Intelligence Review,* (November 23, 2004) 1.

[32] US Department of State, *Trafficking In Persons Report* , 35, 180-182.

[33] "Trafficking in Persons: The U.S. and International Response," By Francis T. Miko, *Congressional Research Service* (Washington D.C.: Library of Congress, July 7, 2006), 2.

[34] "Mexico's Two Border Strategy," *Jane's Intelligence Review* (September 7, 2007), 1.

[35] Miko, "Trafficking in Persons," 8, 18.

[36] "Mexico-United States Dialogue on Migration and Border Issues, 2001-2006," By Colleen W. Cook, *Congressional Research Service* (Washington D.C.: Library of Congress, February 16, 2006), 18.

[37] Weintraub, "The Fence as a Metaphor," 1-2.

[38] "External Affairs, United States," *Jane's Sentinal Security Assessment – North America* (17 October 2008), 21.

[39] *Jane's World Insurgency and Terrorism,* Edited by Tim Pippard (Alexandria, VA: Jane's Information Group Inc., March 2008), 143, 147.

[40] "Fears of Narco-Terrorism Follow Mexico City Blast," *Jane's Intelligence Review* (February 18, 2008), 1.

[41] "Mexican Pipeline Bombers Reject Talks," *Jane's Intelligence Review* (May 8, 2008), 1.

[42] Roderic A. Camp, "Role of Military to Military Cooperation and the Implications and Potential Risks to Civil-Military Relations," Testimony to Congressional Policy Reform, Woodrow Wilson International Center for Scholars (May 9, 2008), 3.

[43] Jay S. Albanese, "Prison Break – Mexican Gang Moves Operations Outside US Jails," *Jane's Intelligence Review* (December 2, 2008), 1.

[44] "Gangs in Central America," By Clare Ribando, *Congressional Research Service* (Washington D.C.: Library of Congress, May 10, 2005), 1-6.

[45] Max G. Manwaring, "Street Gangs: The New Urban Insurgency," (Carlisle Barracks, PA: U.S. Army War College, Strategic Studies Institute, 2005), 1.

[46] Max G. Manwaring, "Gangs, 'Coups D' Streets,' and the New War in Central America" (Carlisle Barracks, PA: U.S. Army War College, Strategic Studies Institute, July 2005), 1-3.

[47] "Injustice and Impunity: Mexico's Flawed Criminal Justice System," (London, United Kingdom: *Amnesty International,* February 7, 2007), 1.

[48] Ibid., 3.

[49] "Guide to Mexican Police Agencies," (Washington, D.C.: Latin American Working Group, 2003), 1.

[50] Ibid.

[51] "Security and Foreign Forces, Mexico," *Jane's Sentinal Security Assessment – Central America and the Caribbean* (February 15, 2008), 2.

[52] "Guide to Mexican Police Agencies," 1.

[53] US Department of Justice, "Law Enforcement Statistics" (Washington D.C., 2004), 1.

[54] "Security and Foreign Forces, Mexico," 1.

[55] Benjamin Reames, "Police Forces in Mexico: A Profile" (La Jolla, CA: Center for U.S. Mexican Studies, May 2003), 8.

Notes

[56] Reames, "Police Forces in Mexico," 7.

[57] "Mexican Authorities Raid Police Headquarters," *Jane's Sentinal Security Assessment – Mexico* (March 19, 2007), 1.

[58] "Mexico Investigates Police Force," *Jane's Sentinal Security Assessment – Mexico* (December 31, 2007), 1.

[59] "Security and Foreign Forces, Mexico," 1.

[60] "Mexico Investigates Police Force," 1.

[61] "Defence Budget, Mexico," *Jane's Sentinal Security Assessment – Central America and the Caribbean* (May 27, 2008), 1.

[62] Jordi Diez and Ian Nicholls, "The Mexican Armed Forces in Transition" (Carlisle Barracks, PA: U.S. Army War College, Strategic Studies Institute, January 2006), 25-26.

[63] Ibid., 38.

[64] Roderic A. Camp, "Civil Military Relations: Charting a New Direction." *Hemisphere Focus* XII, no. 12. (Washington D.C., November 5, 2004), 1, 6.

[65] Diez and Nicholls, "The Mexican Armed Forces in Transition," 41-43.

[66] "Mexico's War Without Rules," 1.

[67] Ken Ellington, "Mexico vs. Drug Gangs: A Deadly Clash for Control," *Los Angeles Times* (Los Angeles, CA, June 3, 2008), 1.

[68] "Mexico's President Defends Military Interventionism," *Janes Intelligence Review-Mexico-Country Risk Daily Report* (May 25, 2008), 1.

[69] Arturo Sotomayor, "Mexico's Armed Forces," *Hemisphere: A Magazine of the Americas* 16 (Spring 2006), 30-31.

[70] Rut Diamint, "Democracy and Defense," *Hemisphere: A Magazine of the Americas* 16 (Spring 2006), 12.

[71] Adam Isacson, Lisa Haugaard, and Joy Olson, "Creeping Militarization in the Americas," *NACLA Report on the Americas* 38 (November/December 2004), 1.

[72] "Section 1206 of the National Defense Authorization Act for FY2006: A Fact Sheet on Department of Defense Authority to Train and Equip Foreign Military Forces," By Nina M. Serafino, *Congressional Research Service* (Washington D.C.: Library of Congress, June 3, 2008), 1.

[73] Roderic A. Camp, "Role of Military to Military Cooperation," 2-5.

[74] US Department of State, *Country Reports on Human Rights Practices - 2007* (Washington D.C.: Released by the Bureau of Democracy, Human Rights, and Labor on March 11, 2008), 1.

[75] "Injustice and Impunity," 1-2.

[76] "Mexico - Unfair Trails: Unsafe Convictions," London, United Kingdom: *Amnesty International* (March 25, 2003), 16.

[77] "Mexico – Amnesty International Submission to the UN Universal Periodic Review, Fourth Session of the UPR Working Group of the Human Rights Council, February 2009" (London, United Kingdom: *Amnesty International,* September 8, 2008), 3.

[78] Joseph L. Klesner, "Electoral Competition and the New Party System in Mexico," *Latin American Politics and Society* 47, no. 2 (Summer 2005), 1, 5, 15.

[79] Ibid., 2, 5, 17.

Notes

[80] Peter DeShazo, "Anticorruption Efforts in Latin America – Lessons Learned," *Policy Papers on the Americas* XVIII, Study 2. (Washington D.C., Center for Strategic and International Studies Americas Program, September 2007), 7.

[81] Luis Rubio and Jeffrey Davidow, "Mexico's Disputed Election," *Foreign Affairs* 85, no. 5 (September/October 2006), 4.

[82] Sidney Weintraub, "Mexico's Presidential Election Was a Significant Event," *Issues In International Political Economy* 79 (Washington, D.C.: Center for Strategic and International Studies, July 2006), 1-2.

[83] "US-Mexico Economic Relations: Trends, Issues, and Implications," By M. Angeles Villareal, *Congressional Research Service* (Washington D.C.: Library of Congress, January 24, 2006), 2.

[84] Ibid., 10.

[85] US Department of Energy, "Country Analysis Briefs: Mexico" (Washington, DC: Energy Information Administration, December 2007), 1.

[86] "US Overseas Loans and Grants [Greenbook]: Mexico," US Agency for International Development, Economic Analysis and Data Services (Accessed December 23, 2008), 1.

[87] "US Direct Investment Abroad: Trends and Current Issues," By James K. Jackson. *Congressional Research Service* (Washington D.C.: Library of Congress, August 15, 2008), 3.

[88] Villareal, "U.S.-Mexico Economic Relations," 2, Table 1.

[89] USDOE, "Country Analysis Briefs: Mexico," 3.

[90] "Index of Economic Freedom 2008 – Mexico," *Heritage.Org.* https://www.heritage.org/index/country.cfm?id=Mexico, 2.

[91] US Senate Committee on Foreign Affairs, *The Merida Initiative: 'Guns, Drugs, and Friends,' 2007*, 110th Congress, 1st Session, 2007 (December 21, 2007), 16-22, 27-28, 33-34.

[92] Ibid., 19-22, 26-27.

[93] Ibid., 54-56, 61-65, 67-72.

[94] Ibid., 22-23, 25-26, 28-29.

[95] Ibid., 56-57.

[96] Ibid., 20-21, 23-25.

[97] Ibid., 57-59, 60-61, 66-67.

[98] Ibid., 39-42.

[99] Ibid., 30-33, 47-49.

[100] Ibid., 73-76.

[101] Ibid., 35-36, 42-46.

[102] Ibid., 29-30, 46-47, 68-69.

[103] US HR 6028, 110th Congress, 2nd Session, 2008. Part III.

[104] US HR 6028, 110th Congress, 2nd Session, 2008. Part IV.

[105] US HR 6028, 110th Congress, 2nd Session, 2008. Part V.

[106] Max G. Manwaring and others, "Building Regional Security Cooperation in the Western Hemisphere: Issues and Recommendations" (Carlisle Barracks, PA: U.S. Army War College. October 2003), V.

[107] Ibid.

Notes

[108] Joseph R. Nunez, "A 21st Century Security Architecture for the Americas: Multilateral Cooperation, Liberal Peace, and Soft Power," (Carlisle Barracks, PA: U.S. Army War College, Strategic Studies Institute, August, 2002), 2-4.

[109] Doug Stokes, *America's Other War: Terrorizing Colombia* (New York: Palgrave Macmillan, 2005), 122-126.

[110] *The Bush Doctrine and Latin America,* Edited by Gary Prevost and Carlos Oliva Campos (New York, NY: Palgrave Macmillan, 2007), 8.

[111] Peter DeShazo, Tanya Primiani, and Phillip McLean, *Back from the Brink: Evaluating Progress in Columbia, 1999-2007* (Washington, D.C.: Center for Strategic and International Studies, Americas Program, 2007), VIII-XI.

[112] Carin Zissis, "President George Bush on U.S. Commitment to the Americas," Council of the Americas, http://www.as-coa.org/, 1.

[113] "International Drug Trade and U.S. Foreign Policy," By Raphael F. Perl, *Congressional Research Service* (Washington D.C.: Library of Congress, July 21, 2006), 12-13.

[114] Alan L. McPherson, *Intimate Ties, Bitter Struggles: The United States and Latin America since 1945*, 1st Edition (Washington: Potomac Books, 2006), 126.

[115] "FY 2008 Federal Drug Budget: Prevention Funding Continues to Decline," (Gaithersburg, MD: Carnevale Associates, LLC., Strategic Policy Solutions, February 2007), 1.

[116] Robert Sherman, "The Real Terrorist Missile Threat," 17.

[117] Matthew Schroeder, *Small Arms, Terrorism, and the OAS Firearms Convention, Federation of American Scientist,* Occasional Paper No. 1 (March 2004), 38.

[118] *Mexico's Democracy at Work: Political and Economic Dynamics,* Edited by Russell Crandall and others (Boulder, London: Lynne Rienner Publishers, 2005), 193.

[119] Max G. Manwaring, *Studies in Asymmetry: Non-state Actors in Columbia-Threat and Response* (Carlisle Barracks, PA: U.S. Army War College, Strategic Studies Institute, May 2002), 11.

[120] US Department of State, "Security and Prosperity Partnership of North America Fact Sheet," The White House (Washington, D.C., March 23, 2005), 1.

[121] Michael Day, "Fourth Dimension – US Revives its Latin American Fleet," *Jane's Intelligence Review* (July 14, 2008), 1.

Bibliography

Addicted to Failure: U.S. Security Policy in Latin America and the Andean Region. Edited by Brian Loveman. Lanham, Maryland: Rowman and Littlefield Publishers, Inc., 2006.

Air University Style Guide for Writers and Editors. Maxwell AFB, AL: Air University Press, April 2005.

Albanese, Jay S. "Prison Break – Mexican Gang Moves Operations Outside US Jails." *Jane's Intelligence Review.* December 2, 2008. http://search.janes.com/Search/document View.do?docId=/content1/janesdata/mags/jir/history/jir2009/jir10528.htm@current&pageSe lected=janesNews&keyword=Mexican%20Gang&backPath=http://search.janes.com/Search &Prod_Name=JIR&.

Ali Camp, Roderic. "Mexico's Military on the Democratic Stage." *Center for Strategic and International Studies.* Westport, CT: Praeger Security International. 2005.

Andreas, Peter. "Politics on Edge: Managing the US-Mexico Border." *Current History* 105 (February 2006). http://proquest.umi.com/pqdweb?did=986385911&sid=5&Fmt=3& clientId=417&RQT=309&VName=PQD.

Arrarás, Astrid, and Deheza, Grace Ivana. "Widening the War on Terror." *Hemisphere: A Magazine of the Americas* 14 (Fall 2004). http://search.ebscohost.com/login.aspx?direct =true&db=aph&AN=5170642&site=ehost-live.

Barone, Michael. "What's Up Down South." *U.S. News & World Report* 140, no. 36 (May 1, 2006). http://search.ebscohost.com/login.aspx?direct=true&db=mth&AN=20558955&site= ehost-live.

Barry, Tom. "Anti-Immigrant Backlash on the 'Home Front'." *NACLA Report on the Americas* 38 (May-June 2005). http://search.ebscohost.com/login.aspx?direct=true&db=aph&AN= 16978323&site=ehost-live.

Beccera, Oscar. "Firing Line – Tracking Mexico's Illegal Weapons." *Jane's Intelligence Review.* May 15, 2008. http://search.janes.com/Search/documentView.do?docId =/content1/janesdata/mags/jir/history/jir2008/jir10393.htm@current&pageSelected=janesNe ws&keyword=mexico%20Weapons&backPath=http://search.janes.com/Search&Prod_Nam e=JIR&.

Becerra, Oscar. "Mexican People-Smuggling Trade Worth Billions." *Jane's Intelligence Review.* November 23, 2004. http://search.janes.com/Search/documentView.do?docId= /content1/janesdata/mags/jir/history/jir2004/jir01128.htm@current&pageSelected=janesNe

ws&keyword=mexico%20smuggling&backPath=http://search.janes.com/Search&Prod_Na
me=JIR&.

Bennett, J. Lee. "A Game of Simon Says: Latin America's Left Turn and Its Effects on U.S. Security." Maxwell AFB, AL: Air Command and Staff College, April 2007. https://www.afresearch.org/skins/RIMS/display.aspx?moduleid= be0e99f3-fc56-4ccb-8dfe-70c0822a153&mode=user&action=researchproject&objectid=080 25294-3be8-4627-9f4b-da10fd798c30.

Benton, Allyson Lucinda. "Mexico's (Temporary) Turn to the Left." *Current History* 105, no. 688 (February 2006). Philadelphia, PA. http://proquest.umi.com/pqdweb?did=986385861&sid=5&Fmt=3&clientId=417&RQT=309&VName=PQD.

Berrigan, Frida. "The U.S. Senate: Stalling Hemispheric Arms Control." *New American Foundation.* (March/April 2008). Washington, D.C. http://www.newamerica.net/publications/articles/2008/u_s_senate_stalling_hemispheric_arms_control.html.

Booth, John A., Wade, Christine J., and Walker, Thomas W. *Understanding Central America: Global Forces, Rebellion, and Change.* Cambridge, MA: Westview Press. 2006.

Buckley, Kevin W. "U.S. Support to Plan Colombia: A Heading Check." Monterey, CA: Naval Postgraduate School. September 2004. http://handle.dtic.mil/100.2/ADA423362.

Burkett, Jeffrey W. "Opening the Mexican Door: Continental Defense Cooperation." Monterey, CA: Naval Postgraduate School. 2005. http://handle.dtic.mil/100.2/ADA439329.

Burton, Fred and Stewart, Scott. "Mexico: Examining Cartel War Violence Through a Protective Intelligence Lens." *Stratfor,* May 14, 2008. http://www.stratfor.com/weekly/mexico_applying_protective_intelligence_lens_cartel_war_violence.

Camp, Roderic A. "Role of Military to Military Cooperation and the Implications and Potential Risks to Civil-Military Relations." Testimony to Congressional Policy Reform. Woodrow Wilson International Center for Scholars. May 9, 2008. http://www.wilson center.org/news/docs/Rod%20Camp%20Military%20Presentation%20WWC.08.pdf.

Camp, Roderic A. "Civil Military Relations: Charting a New Direction." *Hemisphere Focus* XII, no. 12. (Washington D.C., November 5, 2004). http://www.csis.org/component/option,com_csis_pubs/task,view/id,595/type,3/.

Canache, Demarys and Allison, Michael E. "Perception of Political Corruption in Latin American Democracies." *Latin American Politics and Society* 47, no. 3. (Fall 2005). Coral Gables, FL. http://proquest.umi.com/pqdweb?did=882358941&sid=4&Fmt=4&clientId=417&RQT=309&VName=PQD.

Carafano, James J. Ph.D. and Johnson, Stephen. "Strengthening America's Southern Flank Requires a Better Effort." *Backgrounder* 1727 (February 20, 2004). The Heritage Foundation. http://www.heritage.org/Research/HomelandSecurity/bg1727.cfm.

Carlsen, Laura. "A Primer on Plan Mexico." Americas Policy Program Special Report . Washington, DC: Center for International Policy. May 5, 2008, updated July 10, 2008.

Carpenter, Ted Galen. *Bad Neighbor Policy: Washington's Futile War on Drugs in Latin America.* 1st ed. New York: Palgrave MacMillan. 2003.

Castillo Arias, Jaime O. "Information Sharing about International Terrorism in Latin America." Monterey, CA: Naval Postgraduate School. June 2005. http://handle.dtic.mil/100.2/ADA 435495.

Changing Structure of Mexico, Political, Social, and Economic Prospects. 2nd Edition. Edited by Laura Randall. Armonk, NY: M.E. Sharpe. 2006.

"Colombia: Issues for Congress." By Connie Veillette. *Congressional Research Service.* Washington D.C.: Library of Congress. January 19, 2005. http://opencrs.cdt.org/ document/RL32250.

"Comparing Global Influence: China's and U.S. Diplomacy, Foreign Aid, Trade, and Investment in the Developing World." Coordinated by Thomas Lum. *Congressional Research Service.* Washington D.C.: Library of Congress. August 15, 2008. http://opencrs.com/document/ RL34620.

"Contested Presidential Election Undermines Stability in Mexico." *Jane's Intelligence Review.* September 25, 2006. http://search.janes.com/Search/documentView.do?docId=/content1/ janesdata/mags/jir/history/jir2006/jir10031.htm@current&pageSelected=janesNews&keywo rd=Contested%20Presidential%20Election%20mexico&backPath=http://search.janes.com/S earch&Prod_Name=JIR&.

Cope, John A. "A Prescription for Protecting: The Southern Approach." *Joint Force Quarterly JFQ* 42 (Summer 2006). http://www.dtic.mil/doctrine/jel/jfq_pubs/4210.pdf .

Craddock, John and Fick, Barbara R. "The Americas in the 21st Century: The Challenge of Governance and Security." *Joint Force Quarterly JFQ* 42 (Summer 2006). http://www.dtic .mil/doctrine/jel/jfq_pubs/4208.pdf.

Danopoulos, Constantine P. "Economic Measurements and Quality of Life in Mexico." *Journal of Political & Military Sociology* 32 (Winter 2004). http://search.ebscohost.com/ login.aspx?direct=true&db=aph&AN=19403072&site=ehost-live.

Day, Michael. "Fourth Dimension – US Revives its Latin American Fleet." *Jane's Intelligence Review.* July 14, 2008. http://search.janes.com/Search/documentView.do?docId=/content1/

janesdata/mags/jir/history/jir2008/jir10435.htm@current&pageSelected=janesNews&keywo
rd=Fourth%20Dimension&backPath=http://search.janes.com/Search&Prod_Name=JIR&.

*Decentralization, Democratic Governance, and Civil Society in Comparative Perspective:
Africa, Asia, and Latin America.* Edited by Philip Oxhorn and others. Washington:
Woodrow Wilson Center Press. 2004.

"Defence Budget, Mexico." *Jane's Sentinal Security Assessment – Central America and the
Caribbean.* May 27, 2008. http://www.janes.com/.

DeShazo, Peter, Primiani, Tanya, and McLean, Phillip. *Back from the Brink: Evaluating
Progress in Columbia, 1999-2007.* Washington, D.C.: Center for Strategic and
International Studies, Americas Program. 2007.

DeShazo, Peter. "Anticorruption Efforts in Latin America – Lessons Learned." *Policy Papers
on the Americas* XVIII, Study 2. (September 2007) Washington, D.C.: Center for Strategic
and International Studies, Americas Program. http://www.csis.org/media/csis/pubs/070913
_anticorruptionefforts_finalreport.pdf.

Diamint, Rut. "Democracy and Defense." *Hemisphere: A Magazine of the Americas* 16 (Spring
2006). http://search.ebscohost.com/login.aspx?direct=true&db=aph&AN=20195664&site
=ehost-live.

Diez, Jordi and Nicholls, Ian. "The Mexican Armed Forces in Transition." Carlisle Barracks,
PA: U.S. Army War College, Strategic Studies Institute. January 2006. http://handle.
dtic.mil/100.2/ADA442906.

Diminyatz, Kerry L. "Providing for the Common Defense: Securing the Southwest Border."
Carlisle Barracks, PA: U.S. Army War College. 2003. http://handle.dtic.mil/100.2/
ADA414219.

Domínguez, Jorge I. and Fernández de Castro, Rafael. *The United States and Mexico: Between
Partnership and Conflict.* New York: Routledge. 2001.

Dresser, Denise. "Fox's Mexico: Democracy Paralyzed." *Current History* 104, no. 679
(February 2005). http://search.ebscohost.com/login.aspx?direct=true&db=aph&AN
=16143140&site=ehost-live.

Ellington, Ken. "Mexico vs. Drug Gangs: A Deadly Clash for Control." *Los Angeles Times.*
(Los Angeles, CA, June 3, 2008). http://articles.latimes.com/2008/jun/03/world/fg-border3.

"External Affairs, United States." *Jane's Sentinal Security Assessment – North America.* (17
October 2008). http://www.janes.com/.

"Fears of Narco-Terrorism Follow Mexico City Blast." *Jane's Intelligence Review.* (February
18, 2008). http://www.janes.com. Page 1.

Frechette, Myles R. R. Colombia and the United States - The Partnership: But What Is the Endgame? Carlisle Barracks, PA, Strategic Studies Institute, February 2007. http://www.strategicstudiesinstitute.army.mil/pdffiles/PUB762.pdf.

Frechette, Myles R. R. "Rethinking Latin America: A New Approach in US Foreign Policy." *Harvard International Review* 48, no. 2 (Summer 2006). http://web.ebscohost.com/ ehost/detail?vid=10&hid=12&sid=a71fb9a7-8bfe-4e4a-9c9bde5fa2cbb232%40SRCSM2&bdata=JnNpdGU9ZWhvc3QtbGl2ZQ%3d%3d#db=aph& AN=21684954.

"FY 2008 Federal Drug Budget: Prevention Funding Continues to Decline." Gaithersburg, MD: Carnevale Associates, LLC., Strategic Policy Solutions, February 2007.

"Gangs in Central America." By Clare Ribando. *Congressional Research Service*. Washington D.C.: Library of Congress. May 10, 2005. http://handle.dtic.mil/100.2/ADA457336.

Gibbs, Terry. "Democracy's Crisis of Legitimacy in Latin America." *NACLA Report on the Americas* 38, no. 1 (July/August 2004). http://www.globalpolicy.org/socecon develop/ democracy/2004/0704lademocracy.htm.

Giffard, Barnard F. and Wheller, Todd M. "Assisting Professional Militaries in Latin America." Carlisle Barracks, PA: U.S. Army War College, Center for Strategic Leadership. October 2003. http://handle.dtic.mil/100.2/ADA423720.

"Guide to Mexican Police Agencies." Washington, D.C.: Latin American Working Group. 2003. http://www.lawg.org/countries/mexico/police_guide.htm.

Haughian, Shane C. "Plan Columbia: Much More Than a War on Drugs." Maxwell AFB, AL: Air Command and Staff College, April 2007. https://www.afresearch.org/skins/RIMS/ display.aspx?moduleid=be0e99f3-fc56-4ccb-8dfe-670c0822a153&mode=user&action =researchproject&objectid=e9a19621-6166-4fe4-802c-a6a5c753e134.

Holcomb, Trae D. "Securing the Land Border Between the United States and Mexico." Maxwell AFB, AL: Air Command and Staff College, April 2006. https://www.afresearch .org/skins/RIMS/display.aspx?moduleid=be0e99f3-fc56-4ccb-8dfe-670c0822a153&mode =user&action=researchproject&objectid=048790a8-3ecd-4473-bd9c-2855b8b39c44.

Hristov, Jasmin. "Freedom and Democracy or Hunger and Terror: Neoliberalism and Militarization in Latin America." *Social Justice* 32 (2005). http://proquest.umi.com/ pqdweb?did=926638821&Fmt=7&clientId=417&RQT=309&VName=PQD.

"Index of Economic Freedom 2008 – Mexico." *Heritage.Org*. https://www.heritage.org/ index/country.cfm?id=Mexico.

"Injustice and Impunity: Mexico's Flawed Criminal Justice System." London, United Kingdom: *Amnesty International.* February 7, 2007. http://www.amnesty.org/en/library/info/ AMR41/001/2007/en.

"International Drug Trade and U.S. Foreign Policy." By Raphael F. Perl. *Congressional Research Service.* Washington D.C.: Library of Congress. July 21, 2006. http://fpc.state.gov/documents/organization/76892.pdf.

Isacson, Adam, Haugaard, Lisa, and Olson, Joy. "Creeping Militarization in the Americas." *NACLA Report on the Americas* 38 (November/December 2004). http://search. ebscohost.com/login.aspx?direct=true&db=aph&AN=15155698&site=ehost-live.

Isacson, Adam. "Closing the "Seams": U.S. Security Policy in the Americas." *NACLA Report on the Americas* 38 (May-June 2005). http://search.ebscohost.com/login.aspx?direct =true&db=aph&AN=16978263&site=ehost-live.

Jane's World Insurgency and Terrorism. Edited by Tim Pippard. Jane's Information Group Inc., Alexandria, VA. March 2008.

Klesner, Joseph L. "Electoral Competition and the New Party System in Mexico." *Latin American Politics and Society* 47, no. 2 (Summer 2005). http://proquest.umi.com/ pqdweb?did=834474651&sid=3&Fmt=4&clientId=417&RQT=309&VName=PQD.

Latin America in a Changing Global Environment. Edited by Riordan Roett and Guadalupe Paz. Boulder, CO: Lynne Reinner. 2003.

Leogrande, William M. "A Poverty of Imagination: George W. Bush's Policy in Latin America." *Journal of Latin American Studies* 39 (May 2007). http://journals.cambridge. org/action/displayAbstract?fromPage=online&aid=1005176&previous=true&jid=LAS&vol umeId=39&issueId=02.

Livingstone, Grace. *Inside Colombia: Drugs, Democracy and War.* New Brunswick, NJ: Rutgers University Press. 2004.

Longhurst, Ricky M. and Lopez, Jesus K. "The Forgotten Insurgency: Is There Hope for Colombia?" Monterey, CA: Naval Postgraduate School. 2005. http://handle.dtic.mil/ 100.2/ADA443320.

Manwaring, Max G. and others. "Building Regional Security Cooperation in the Western Hemisphere: Issues and Recommendations." Carlisle Barracks, PA: U.S. Army War College. October 2003. http://www.carlisle.army.mil/ssi/pdffiles/00004.pdf.

Manwaring, Max G. "Street Gangs: The New Urban Insurgency." Carlisle Barracks, PA: U.S. Army War College, Strategic Studies Institute. 2005. http://www.carlisle.army.mil/ssi/ pdffiles/PUB597.pdf.

Manwaring, Max G. "The Challenge of Governance and Security." Carlisle Barracks, PA: U.S. Army War College, Strategic Studies Institute. 2006. http://handle.dtic.mil/100.2/ADA446771.

Manwaring, Max G. *Studies in Asymmetry: Non-state Actors in Columbia-Threat and Response.* Carlisle Barracks, PA: U.S. Army War College, Strategic Studies Institute. May 2002.

Manwaring, Max. Gangs, "'Coups D' Streets,'" and the New War in Central America." Carlisle Barracks, PA: U.S. Army War College, Strategic Studies Institute. July 2005. http://handle.dtic.mil/100.2/ADA435414.

McLean, Jeffrey E. "U.S. Drug Control Policy's Second and Third Order Effects on Colombia: Destabilizing Democracy and Fostering Narco-Terrorism." Carlisle Barracks, PA: U.S. Army War College. 2005. http://handle.dtic.mil/100.2/ADA432291.

McPherson, Alan L. *Intimate Ties, Bitter Struggles: The United States and Latin America since 1945.* 1st Edition. Washington: Potomac Books. 2006.

"Mérida Initiative: Proposed U.S. Anticrime and Counterdrug Assistance for Mexico and Central America." By Colleen W. Cook, Rebecca G. Rush, and Clare R. Seelke. *Congressional Research Service.* Washington D.C.: Library of Congress. June 3, 2008. http://digital.library.unt.edu/govdocs/crs/permalink/meta-crs-10730:1.

"Mexican Authorities Raid Police Headquarters." *Jane's Sentinal Security Assessment – Mexico.* March 19, 2007. http://search.janes.com/Search/documentView.do?docId=/content1/janesdata/mags/iwr/history/iwr2007/iv14n055d.htm@current&pageSelected=janesNews&keyword=Raid%20Police%20mexico&backPath=http://search.janes.com/Search&Prod_Name=IWR&.

"Mexican Drug Cartels: Government Progress and Growing Violence." *Stratfor.* December 11, 2008. http://www.stratfor.com/analysis/20081209_mexican_drug_cartels_government_progress_and_growing_violence.

"Mexican Pipeline Bombers Reject Talks." *Jane's Intelligence Review.* (May 8, 2008). http://www.janes.com.

Mexico: 2008 Country Review. Edited by Denise Y. Coleman Ph.D. Houston, TX: Country Watch, Inc. 2008. http://www.countrywatch.com.

"Mexico – Amnesty International Submission to the UN Universal Periodic Review, Fourth Session of the UPR Working Group of the Human Rights Council, February 2009." London, United Kingdom: *Amnesty International.* September 8, 2008. http://www.amnesty.org/en/library/info/AMR41/038/2008/en.

"Mexico Investigates Police Force." *Jane's Sentinal Security Assessment – Mexico.* December 31, 2007. http://search.janes.com/Search/documentView.do?docId=/content1/janesdata/

mags/iwr/history/iwr2008/iv15n001d.htm@current&pageSelected=janesNews&keyword=M
exico%20Investigates%20Police%20Force&backPath=http://search.janes.com/Search&Prod
_Name=IWR&.

"Mexico: Ring of Cartel Moles in Key Anti-Narco Positions." *Security and Strategic Review*.
(October 2008). http://www.latinnews.com/lss/LSS19804.asp?Instance =10.

"Mexico - Unfair Trails: Unsafe Convictions." London, United Kingdom: *Amnesty
International*. March 25, 2003. http://www.amnesty.org/en/library/info/AMR41/
007/2003/en.

"Mexico-U.S. Relations: Issues for Congress." By Mark P. Sullivan, Colleen W. Cook, and
Alessandra Durand. *Congressional Research Service*. Washington D.C.: Library of
Congress. November 14, 2008. http://opencrs.com/document/RL32724.

Mexico's Democracy at Work: Political and Economic Dynamics. Edited by Russell Crandall
and others. Boulder, London: Lynne Rienner Publishers. 2005.

"Mexico's Destabilized by Weapons from US." *Jane's Intelligence Review*. December 11,
2007. http://search.janes.com/Search/documentView.do?docId=/content1/janesdata/mags/
iwr/history/iwr2007/iv14n241b.htm@current&pageSelected=janesNews&keyword=Weapo
ns%20mexico&backPath=http://search.janes.com/Search&Prod_Name=IWR&.

"Mexico's President Defends Military Interventionism." *Janes Intelligence Review-Mexico-
Country Risk Daily Report*. May 25, 2008. http://search.janes.com/Search/
documentView.do?docId=/content1/janesdata/mags/iwr/history/iwr2007/iv14n101a.htm@cu
rrent&pageSelected=janesNews&keyword=Military%20Interventionism&backPath=http://s
earch.janes.com/Search&Prod_Name=IWR&.

"Mexico's Two Border Strategy." *Jane's Intelligence Review*. September 7, 2007.
http://search.janes.com/Search/documentView.do?docId=/content1/janesdata/mags/jid/histor
y/jid2007/jid70195.htm@current&pageSelected=janesNews&keyword=Mexico%20Border
%20Strategy&backPath=http://search.janes.com/Search&Prod_Name=JID&.

"Mexico's War Without Rules." *Janes Intelligence Review-Americas-Foreign Report.* May 16,
2008. http://search.janes.com/Search/documentView.do?docId=/content1/janesdata/
mags/frp/history/frp2008/frp70535.htm@current&pageSelected=janesNews&keyword=Mex
ico%20War&backPath=http://search.janes.com/Search&Prod_Name=FREP&.

"Mexico-United States Dialogue on Migration and Border Issues, 2001-2006." By Colleen W.
Cook. *Congressional Research Service*. Washington D.C.: Library of Congress. February
16, 2006. http://digital.library.unt.edu/govdocs/crs/permalink/meta-crs-9372:1.

Meyer, Maureen, Youngers, Coletta and Bewley-Taylor, Dave. "At a Crossroads: Drug
Trafficking, Violence, and the Mexican State." Washington Office of Latin America:

Briefing Paper Thirteen. November 2007. http://www.wola.org/media/Beckley%20 Briefing13web%20(2).pdf.

Millet, Richard L. "Limits of Influence: Creating Security Forces in Latin America." Joint Forces Quarterly 42 (Summer, 2006). http://www.dtic.mil/doctrine/jel/jfq_pubs/4209.pdf.

Nunez, Joseph R. "A 21st Century Security Architecture for the Americas: Multilateral Cooperation, Liberal Peace, and Soft Power." Carlisle Barracks, PA: U.S. Army War College, Strategic Studies Institute. August, 2002. http://handle.dtic.mil/100.2/ADA 405940.

"OAS Convention Against Illicit Firearms Trafficking Fact Sheet." The White House, Office of the Press Secretary. November 14, 1997. http://www.fas.org/asmp/resources/ govern/oasillicit.html.

Office of the President of the United States. *The National Security Strategy of the United States of America*. Washington, D.C. March 2006.

Olsen, Eric. "Six Key Issues in United States-Mexico Security Cooperation." Woodrow Wilson International Center for Scholars. July 2008. http://www.wilsoncenter.org/news/docs/ Olson%20Brief.pdf.

Pion-Berlin, David S. "Political Management of the Military in Latin America." *Military Review* 85 (January/February 2005). http://search.ebscohost.com/login.aspx?direct =rue& db=aph&AN=16241303&site=ehost-live.

Reames, Benjamin. "Police Forces in Mexico: A Profile." La Jolla, CA: Center for U.S. Mexican Studies. May 2003. http://repositories.cdlib.org/cgi/viewcontent.cgi?Article =1025 &context=usmex.

Rios-Figueroa, Julio. "Fragmentation of Power and the Emergence of an Effective Judiciary in Mexico, 1994-2002." *Latin American Politics and Society* 49 (Spring 2007). http://search. ebscohost.com/login.aspx?direct=true&db=aph&AN=24402788&site=ehost-live.

Roett, Riordan and Paz, Guadalupe. *Latin America in a Changing Global Environment*. Boulder, CO: Lynne Reinner Publishers. 2003.

Rozental, Andres. "The Other Side of Immigration." *Current History* 106 (February 2007). http://www.currenthistory.com/Article.php?ID=458.

Rubio, Luis and Davidow, Jeffrey. "Mexico's Disputed Election." *Foreign Affairs.* 85, no. 5 (September/October 2006). http://search.ebscohost.com/login.aspx?direct=true& db=aph&AN=22049790&site=ehost-live.

Schroeder, Matthew. *Small Arms, Terrorism, and the OAS Firearms Convention. Federation of American Scientists.* Occasional Paper No. 1. March 2004. http://www.smallarmssurvey .org/files/portal/issueareas/measures/Measur_pdf/Schroeder%20OAS%20Convention.pdf.

"Section 1206 of the National Defense Authorization Act for FY2006: A Fact Sheet on Department of Defense Authority to Train and Equip Foreign Military Forces." By Nina M. Serafino. *Congressional Research Service.* Washington D.C.: Library of Congress. June 3, 2008. http://assets.opencrs.com/rpts/RS22855_20081125.pdf.

"Security and Foreign Forces, Mexico." *Jane's Sentinal Security Assessment – Central America and the Caribbean.* February 15, 2008. http://www.janes.com/.

Selee, Andrew. "Overview of the Mérida Initiative." Woodrow Wilson International Center for Scholars, May 2008. http://www.wilsoncenter.org/news/docs/Analysis.Merida%20Initiative %20May%208%202008.pdf.

Sherman, Robert. "The Real Terrorist Missile Threat and What Can Be Done About It." *Federation of American Scientists* 56, no. 3 (Autumn 2003).

Sipri Yearbook: World Armaments and Disarmament. New York: Stockholm International Peace Research Institute, Almquist & Wiksell, Humanities Press. 2006.

Sotomayor, Arturo. "Mexico's Armed Forces." *Hemisphere: A Magazine of the Americas.* 16 (Spring 2006). http://search.ebscohost.com/login.aspx?direct=true&db=aph&AN= 20195671&site=ehost-live.

Spinetta, Lawrence J. "Strengthening North American Security: A Strategy to Engage Mexico." Maxwell AFB, AL: Air Command and Staff College, April 2005. https://www.afresearch.org/skins/RIMS/display.aspx?moduleid=be0e99f3-fc56-4ccb-8dfe-670c0822a153&mode=user&action=lresearch&objectid=e427d592-acd8-47cd-a6a7-7d467250f74f.

Staats, Joseph L. and others. "Measuring Judicial Performance in Latin America." *Latin American Politics and Society* 47 (Winter 2005). http://proquest.umi.com/ pqdweb?did=950430921&sid=1&Fmt=4&clientId=417&RQT=309&VName=PQD.

Stokes, Doug. *America's Other War: Terrorizing Colombia.* New York: Palgrave Macmillan. 2005.

Taylor, Paul B. "Latin American Security Challenges: A Collaborative Inquiry from North and South." Newport, RI: U.S. Naval War College. 2004.

The Bush Doctrine and Latin America. Edited by Gary Prevost and Carlos Oliva Campos. New York, NY: Palgrave Macmillan. 2007.

"Trafficking in Persons: The U.S. and International Response." By Francis T. Miko. *Congressional Research Service.* Washington D.C.: Library of Congress. July 7, 2006. http://www.usembassy.it/pdf/other/RL30545.pdf.

Turner, Barry. *Latin America Profiled: Essential Facts on Society, Business, and Politics in Latin America.* New York, NY: St. Martin's Press. 2000.

Ungar, Mark. *Elusive Reform: Democracy and the Rule of Law in Latin America.* Boulder, CO: Lynne Rienner Publishers. 2002.

US Department of Defense. *National Military Strategy of the United States of America.* Washington, DC: Department of Defense. May 2004.

US Department of Defense. *National Defense Strategy of the United States of America.* Washington, DC: Department of Defense. June 2008.

US Department of Defense. *National Military Strategic Plan for the War on Terrorism.* Washington DC: Office of the Secretary of Defense. 2006.

US Department of Defense. *Quadrennial Defense Review Report.* Washington, DC: Department of Defense. February 2006.

US Department of Energy. "Country Analysis Briefs: Mexico." Washington, DC: Energy Information Administration. December 2007. http://www.eia.doe.gov/emeu/cabs/Mexico/pdf.pdf.

US Department of Justice. "Law Enforcement Statistics." Washington D.C. 2004. http://ojp.usdoj.gov/bjs/lawenf.htm.

US Department of Justice. *National Drug Threat Assessment.* Washington D.C.: National Drug Intelligence Center. 2009. http://www.usdoj.gov/ndic/topics/ndtas.htm.

US Department of State. *Country Reports on Human Rights Practices - 2007.* The White House, Washington D.C.: Released by the Bureau of Democracy, Human Rights, and Labor on March 11, 2008. http://www.stste.gov/g/drl/rls/hrrpt/2007/100646.htm.

US Department of State. "Security and Prosperity Partnership of North America Fact Sheet." The White House, Washington, D.C., March 23, 2005.

US Department of State. *Trafficking In Persons Report.* The White House, Washington, D.C., June 2008. http://www.state.gov/g/tip/rls/tiprpt/2008/.

"US Direct Investment Abroad: Trends and Current Issues." By James K. Jackson. *Congressional Research Service.* Washington D.C.: Library of Congress. August 15, 2008. http://opencrs.com/document/RS21118/2006-04-26.

"US Drug Trafficking Report: Part II." *Central America Report* 33 (March 17, 2006).

US Embassy Mexico City. "Combating Illicit Firearms." September 2008. http://www.us embassy-mexico.gov/eng/eataglance_illicit_firearms.pdf.

"US Foreign Assistance to Latin America and the Caribbean." Coordinated by Connie Veillette and others. *Congressional Research Service.* Washington D.C.: Library of Congress. March 30, 2005. http://www.ncseonline.org/nle/crsreports/05mar/RL32487.pdf

US General Accounting Office. "Drug Control: Efforts to Develop Alternatives to Cultivating Illicit Crops in Colombia Have Made Little Progress and Face Serious Obstacles." Washington D.C.: GAO. 2002. http://handle.dtic.mil/100.2/ADA399261.

US General Accounting Office. "U.S. Assistance Has Helped Mexican Counternarcotics Efforts, but the Flow of Illicit Drugs into the United States Remains High." Washington D.C.: GAO. US House, 110th Congress, 1st Session, October 25, 2007.

US House Committee on Foreign Affairs, *Merida Initiative to Combat Illicit Narcotics and Reduce Organized Crime Authorization Act of 2008*, 2008: Report to accompany HR 6028, prepared by Hon. Howard Burman, 110th Congress, 2nd Session, 2008, May 22, 2008.

US House Committee on Government Reform. *The Study of Plan Columbia: An Assessment of Successes and Challenges.* Hearing. 107th Congress, 1st Session, March 2, 2001.

US House Committee on Government Reform. *The War Against Drugs and Thugs: A Status Report on Plan Colombia Successes and Remaining Challenges.* Hearing. 108th Congress, 2nd Session, June 17, 2004. Washington, GPO, June 17, 2004. http://purl.access. gpo.gov/GPO/LPS58351.

US HR 6028, 110th Congress, 2nd Session, 2008.

"US Overseas Loans and Grants [Greenbook]: Mexico." US Agency for International Development. Economic Analysis and Data Services. Accessed December 23, 2008. https://qesdb.usaid.gov/cgi-bin/broker.exe.

US Senate Committee on Foreign Affairs, *The Merida Initiative: 'Guns, Drugs, and Friends,' 2007*, 110th Congress, 1st Session, 2007, December 21, 2007.

US Senate Committee on Foreign Relations. *Challenges and Successes for U.S. Policy Toward Colombia: Is Plan Columbia Working?* 108th Congress, 1st Session, 2003, October 29, 2003. http://purl.access. gpo.gov/GPO/LPS50853.

US Senate Committee on Foreign Relations. *U.S.-Columbia Policy: What's Next?* 107th Congress, 2nd Session, 2002, April 24, 2002.

"US-Latin America Trade: Recent Trends." By J.F. Hornbeck and Marisabel Cid. *Congressional Research Service.* Washington D.C.: Library of Congress. July 18, 2008. http://opencrs.com/document/98-840.

"US-Mexico Economic Relations: Trends, Issues, and Implications." By M. Angeles Villareal. *Congressional Research Service.* Washington D.C.: Library of Congress. January 24, 2006. http://opencrs.com/document/RL32934/2005-05-25.

Walker, William J. "The Relationship and Threat of Transnational Organized Crime, Drug Traffickers and Terrorist Groups in the Western Hemisphere: The Hot Spots." Washington, Inter American Defense College. April 2006. http://library.jid.org/en/ mono45/Walker.pdf.

Walser, Ray, Ph.D. "Latin America and the U.S.: Building a Partnership for the Western Hemisphere." *Backgrounder* 2238 (February 5, 2009). The Heritage Foundation. http://www.heritage.org/Research/LatinAmerica/bg2238.cfm.

Walser, Ray, Ph.D. "Mexico, Drug Cartels, and the Mérida Initiative: A Fight We Cannot Afford to Lose." *Backgrounder* 2163 (July 23, 2008). The Heritage Foundation. http://www.heritage.org/Research/LatinAmerica/bg2163.cfm.

Walser, Ray, Ph.D. and Roberts, James M. "The U.S. and Mexico: Taking the Mérida Initiative Against Narco-Terrorism." *Backgrounder* 1705 (November 16, 2007). The Heritage Foundation. http://www.heritage.org/Research/LatinAmerica/bg2163.cfm.

Weintraub, Sidney. "Mexico's Presidential Election Was a Significant Event." *Issues In International Political Economy* 79. Washington, D.C.: Center for Strategic and International Studies. July 2006. http://www.csis.org/index.php?option=com_csis_pubs &task=view&id=3361.

Weintraub, Sidney. "The Fence as a Metaphor for How the United States Views Its Relations with Mexico." *Issues In International Political Economy* 82. Washington, D.C.: Center for Strategic and International Studies. October 2006. http://www.csis.org/index.php?option= com_csis_pubs&task=view&id=3540.

Wiarda, Howard J. *Dilemmas of Democracy in Latin America.* Lanham, Maryland: Rowman and Littlefield Publishers, Inc. 2005.

Youngers, Coletta and Rosin, Eileen. *Drugs and Democracy in Latin America: The Impact of U.S. Policy.* Boulder, CO: Lynne Rienner Publishers. 2005.

Zissis, Carin. "President George Bush on U.S. Commitment to the Americas." Council of the Americas. http://www.as-coa.org/.